STAR

poems
for the
Christmas Season

Angela Graham
images by Martin Erspamer

thanks & acknowledgements

My thanks first and foremost to poet and publisher, Phil Cope whose generosity, skill and insight are crucial to this book; and to poet, Julian Cason, an essential critical reader of my work. I am profoundly grateful to Martin Erspamer OSB who has generously allowed me to enhance the collection with his wonderful images. I have greatly appreciated the encouragement of poet, Damian Smyth, Head of Literature and Drama at the Arts Council of Northern Ireland.

My husband, John Geraint and my children, Róisín, Seán and Anwen have given me many happy Christmases. Their love and support are the mainstay of my writing.

As a poet, I don't write alone but with an awareness of the fellowship of poets around me, whose dedication to the craft is a constant inspiration. Particular thanks for help with Irish to Réaltán Ní Leannáin, with Scots to Stuart Paterson, and with Braid Ulster-Scots to Ashley Todd. Thank you all.

Special thanks to rheumatologist, Dr Sharon Jones and her colleagues in the NHS.

Several poems in this collection were previously published by Black Bough Poems, Grey Hen Press, The Lonely Crowd, Words From The Brink (Arachne Press), The Bangor Literary Journal and Amethyst Review. Five of the poems were featured in BBC Radio Wales' *A Christmas Meditation* programme on Christmas Eve 2023.

© **Angela Graham** second edition November 2024
https://angelagraham.org/

images © Martin Erspamer OSB

ISBN: 978-1-0686946-0-8

a *culture & democracy press* publication
https://tinyurl.com/CultureAndDemocracyPress

foreword

The Christmas season – six weeks or so of lead-up and celebration – ends with the Epiphany on the 6th January (Twelfth Night). This commemorates the Three Kings – or Magi, or Wise Men – who find the infant Jesus in Bethlehem.

In these poems those three men 'from the east' are prominent, as protagonists but also as figures who embody our own daily search for something meaningful. The Three Kings, I imagine here, had Queens. Every powerful story, even when it's as well known as the Christmas one, leaves room for *What if? What next? Who else?* The Three Queens and Three Kings are at the heart of this book.

Christmas touches into our deepest hopes and fears at the time of year when life is most vulnerable – during these weeks the Old Year dies, and the New Year is born. Profound things emerge in ordinary settings; homely rituals are transformed by the unexpected, the shocking, the tragic, the marvellous ...

And the star – aspiration, guidance, inspiration, hope – travels with us.

Merry Christmas!

Angela Graham

CHRISTMAS RESOLUTION

This year – this year – to be
as given as a newborn;
my simplest, giving, self.

CHRISTMAS

The smallest words mean the most

      Joy

      Hope

      Love

These things

Not things

May you receive them all:

      A star   of particular promise

      A light   that has sought and found you

      The child   of your heart

Arrived

Waiting beyond the door.

SHINING

Those greens of winter – the holly, ivy and the hellebore –
gleam and the lighted window, beaming across the waste,
is an eye looking out for us. Whatever shines, sees:
the burnish on polished furniture, the glow of brass,
the pristine glint of a windowpane; all things
caressed with care give back that tenderness;
tell us they'd miss us if we weren't there.

So, when I drape the lights around the Christmas tree,
dot it with tinsel, baubles and shiny fripperies, and set it
– gorgeous – in the front-room window, it's for you to see
as you walk around the corner out of Mortimer Road;
for you to know my heart is gazing – less ostentatiously –
along the street, waiting for you; reflecting
your brightness, your warmth, your cherishing.

NEWS

Delighted with herself and four years old,
she has a secret for me; whispers gleefully,
It's going to be Christmas. AGAIN!

I won't tell anyone, I promise.
But somehow word gets out.
Fairy lights in the neighbours' windows.

Once is never enough.
We have a need to tell each other every year
that we will always make room;

that if things don't go as planned there'll be
enough to get by, and that fulfilment
– our birthright – is coming, laden with gifts.

READING CHRISTMAS POEMS

I read about a fox padding on snow,
water freezing in pails in the corner of a farmyard,
the moon a plate of ice propped on a high, high shelf.

But my Christmas is a city one.
The sky at night's no higher than the street-lamps;
bumper-to-bumper the cars churr on the main road
and snarl or sigh in this narrow thoroughfare
and it mostly rains, is damply chill.

The house is old, but new to me. I've just moved in.
Still trying to find a place for things.
Across the street a family's white Christmas tree
glistens in their first-floor window;
their neighbour's run a string of beaming cherries
all along his railings; next door to me
they've put some twinkling baubles
among window pots of puce and purple cyclamen.

I don't know any of these people yet
but in the early darkness that lovely tree
fills to perfection the top right pane
of the sash in my front sitting room.

It's fitting that the angels sang in the open countryside
but maybe someone, in the over-crowded streets nearby,
looked up and heard
the stillness
when they drew breath
between each stanza of their praise.

THE CHRISTMAS CARD

For years, a Christmas card would come
for people several owners back,
addressed in an elderly hand
with a *Season's Greetings. Love from ...*
Even I forget the name. Never a return address.
It got so I'd look out for it,
hoping for some way to answer.
The year arrived when no card came.
And, of course, never again.

Come all ye faithful tenders of faint flames,
semaphoring valiantly
across the year-long dark;
doing all your part to keep a link alive;
insisting you be seen
(if only by the Royal Mail and me);
insisting your Christmas message
would be missed.
Such dignity.

CHRISSMAS EVE

A'm scunnerd – iverie year – whun thair's me,
Chrissmas Eve, swep up agane in tha yin aul margymore,
empied, sumhoo – o money, aye – but o some ither thaing
– pains me ahlmost – sumthin A hae loast.

An then A seen er, stannin fernenst a reck o claes,
her babbie in er airms. A doot if she heerd a peep
in tha wile millee aroon her – shappin, ganshin, gulderin –
she wus that tuk wae'm.

Tha manysther saes tha Sinn o God wull come
in pooer an glory, cloods reevit, tha sea aboil
an tha stars teemed oot o haiven,
skailt lik leaves frae a crinnelt tree.

A must mine an tell him whut A seen theday
in Marks an Spencers in Ballameena,
hoo He come, whun A wusnae even lukkin for Him,
tae gie me tha fu o m' heart.

Ulster-Scots:

scunnerd – completely fed up
tha yin aul margymore –
the same old chaotic crowd
empied – emptied
fernenst a reck o claes –
by a clothes rack
wile millee – very unruly crowd
ganshin, gulderin – chatting,
yelling

tuk wae'm - absorbed in him
manysther - clergyperson
Sinn o God - Son of God
reevit - torn apart
teemed - poured
mine - remember
skailt - scattered
crinnelt - wrinkled
theday - today
gie me tha fu o m' heart –
fill my heart completely

IN THE SHOPPING ARCADES

What are you carrying
through this arcade?
Here, you are sheltered, so
consider:
a broken heart,
or a heart with wings;
a burden
or a treasure?

And you yourself, a gift,
passing the shopfronts, reflected,
are you one of the everyday magi
threading the city
with the myrrh of compassion,
the perfume of hope
and the gold you've refined from sharp sorrow?

What are you carrying
through this arcade?

What do you want to lay down
or take up?

What is it carries you
through this arcade?

WHAT THE STARS WANT TO TELL US

The stars, a rowdy, cheerful crowd,
ran to their places, prompt to the call,
and how they sing! since then,
a nightly choir.
Only the comets, their slow tears,
betray the sorrow underneath that steadfastness
for haven't they seen it all?
– what we do down here,
warping the darkness that they love
into sly coverts for our filthiness.
Poor stars. Don't grudge them their reprieve
each year, when their paragon,
their Star of stars, leader of kings,
sets out once more and triumphs,
finds his place, finding the child,
perfect as every newborn.
Here! the Star declares to each of us,
Surely you see – surely – that you
are a Child Awaited,
arrived, naked and beloved, and you,
gift-bearer of nothing,
can stoop under the lintel,
step clean through the needle's eye.

AUTUN CATHEDRAL, MAGI

Does the sky have tent-poles?

And some cathedrals are forested.
God walks in their depths on a December afternoon
while the topmost branches brush the undersides
of planets fixed mid-orbit
      – those stained-glass windows fruiting overhead.
Here no one thinks of weight, of downwardness
and how the roof desires it.

God pauses among the pillars
at a carved capital that always lifts his heart:

an artist like himself, from this blunt-cornered oblong stone,
gives us a bird's view of a bed
draped in a ruched counterpane, three kings tucked in,
but the eyes of one, popped open, register
Why? Who? still unaware
of the angel at his shoulder, stroking his hand,
whose other index finger points at a star.

God sighs, at the weight borne by the moment
after such a moment; at how he waits
for a man to look up at the sky
and recognise and seize
the chance of joy.

THREE KINGS

BALTHAZAR

When the roads turned into streets
and the streets to lanes
and the lanes to alleys
I became suspicious.
I suspected ...
... something we had not prepared for.

Our retinue had fallen more and more behind
as I stepped into a passageway between high walls
like a certain defile in the mountainous lands
where even an army is funnelled down
to a chain of individual men,
each painfully aware
of his life as a single flame
fluttering in the lantern of his body
and carried forward only as his flesh and blood allows;
instinctively, each one looks up,
to check the sky's still there,
that he hasn't been shut inside
that long and narrow tomb.

I did the same.
There was the star,
framed in the gap above me,
majestically insistent we press on.

An animal tang grew stronger
and lantern light somewhere ahead
and voices
and Caspar and Melchior stooped to the left
and vanished through a shabby stable door, and I –
I was made to feel ashamed
of my gift – ostentatious,
my crown – ludicrous,
my glittering clothes.
And I did not – could not – kneel with the others,
their faces tender and self-forgetful.

We sought kingship and were given this!
How could such a child acquire what a king must have:
authority, and power to sway all to his will?

Then the mother (calm, tired) looked up at me,
her gaze a chalice into which my anger poured,
seething, rocking against itself from rim to rim.
That is what I brought her – bitterness.
She felt it. Accepted it. She raised the child towards me.
I thrust my gift aside and took him
– her gift to me. I held his life
and she refused to let fear rule her.
Sovereignty. Autonomy. And might.

MELCHIOR

We see.
We see significance.
We know enough to know there's something to be known.

The three of us on a balcony at night,
looking away from ourselves
to the vast otherness of the skies,

looked to a presence – signalled by the placement of those lights,
their shifts (like pieces swept across a board),
their seasonal predictabilities –

to a presence which insisted on a meaning
that would be plain to us
if we were pure enough.

I was the first to point to that particular star.
I'd dreamt about a torch, pushing the darkness back
towards the west,

towards a meeting of some portentous kind
and we agreed this was a star of voyage
and arrival; of revelation at the journey's end.

When we reached that humble, marvellous place, Caspar was rapt
and Balthazar indignant, then heart-shaken; both
feeling too much to see what I saw suddenly, next day,

that every birth brings blood and we,

dazzled by our heady search, had failed to see

that there can never be two kings on an earthly throne.

Pawns in King Herod's hand, we were;

path-finders for his murderous intent.

There was no time to reason

so I lied. A mighty dream, I claimed, had let me see

we must go back by another route.

At once. In secret.

What else would have torn them away?

Then, chaos and hugger-mugger;

retreat, humiliation, waste

and shame. For we escaped. But that mother, father, baby?

How I've prayed the young husband dreamt, that night,

of flight, of refuge sought, of sanctuary.

CASPAR

I am too old now to keep a vigil from anywhere but my bed.
I watch the constellations roll with infinite slowness
past my un-shuttered window. I raise my face
to the cold radiance of the late spring sky and ask to be forgiven.
"My friends," I say to Balthazar and Melchior. And I say nothing more.
They are dead. I am still watching. What else would any of us do?

We made a very great mistake. Despite our learning,
our capacity to read the subtle dispositions overhead;
despite being each of us a king, we failed to allow for the way
a king's mind works. We must have expected praise, and Herod, that fox,
lavished his astonishment that we had tracked on the humble earth
the pathway of a star. We told him we thought only of the search
but each (to himself) pictured the fame awaiting
men so clever they found the whole world's turning point.

Fools would have kept their counsel – and the child –
then judged who to tell and when. We, guilty men, escaped,
while the co-ordinates we gave up so naively
fuelled the lethal search for that infant king.

Tonight, three decades later, why is his star
suddenly brilliant in the east, as though
our faults have not disrupted the equation, as though
they have been aligned with his ascendant, as though
he has come into his kingdom ...? As though
mercy is the hand turning that wheel.

THREE QUEENS

THE WIFE OF BALTHAZAR

Child bride; Parthian princess
(who had never been or seen
anywhere or anything beyond her parents' court);
dynastic socket he fitted himself into
for the kingdom's sake.
His passion was the stars.

So he failed to see her sapling-growth
out-stripping and out-thinking him
till the day he entered her apartments unannounced
and, though the pool of women laughing settled at once,
he glimpsed, beneath her deferential bow,
a tiny smile:
the corner of a curtain just not quite pulled to.

Five years and still no child.
He had her watched.

They told him she had learned to read and write and count;
that she stood by the physicians as they set and un-set bones
and followed their servants in the gardens choosing herbs;
that she liked to be where she could hear the interpreters of dreams
sifting their catch and lawyers weighing evidence and accusation;

that she had been seen lifting his astrolabe,

had run her fingers over its precious indentations

and later asked a judge which laws

govern the stars.

Why did she not ask me?

Now she came between him and the skies;

his new heaven

beneath him in the bed,

always receding,

a spark unreachable.

Caspar counselled, *Talk to her.*

He spoke of the zodiac, of calendars, eclipses, mathematics

and he watched her smile brighten, widen,

till her eyes unveiled themselves.

I am tearing myself apart, he told her,

when he had to leave

on the long quest westward.

You are my star!

When he returned,

breathless to tell her of that birth,

the heralds met him at the border:

You have a son. The queen is dead.

MELCHIOR'S QUEEN

He'd been home for ages
and I hadn't been able to get him
to tell me anything much about her.

He came back
to everything
running exactly as it should.

Why wouldn't it?
I was in charge
and I can make men jump.

Innovations? Oh yes.
Improvements. Some promotions.
Some dead wood gone.

Sharper all round. He said so.
I said, *What's the point of power*
if you can't get what you want?

So, he'd talk about the child
but when I asked about the mother
he went vague. Evasive. Guilty?

I did go on
and on and on
just because he wouldn't tell me.

Tried the usuals:
cajoling, pouting, temper,
temptress …

Finally, last night,
after he'd made love to me
in a very particular way …

he took me onto the terrace.
Look up there, he said.
What do you see?

I did my best.
I didn't say, *Just the usual,*
Let's go back to bed.

I said, *Stars, my darling.*
The moon.
He asked, *What else?*

I tell you,
it was cold by this time
so I was sharpish, saying, *More stars?*

He said, *The sky.*
Yes, yes. And so …?
These intellectuals!

She was like that, he says,
his face tilted up,
yearning.

Never let them yearn.
The only one they should be pining for
is you. In this case, me.

So I opened my mouth
to let him have it
and he says,

She was a midnight sky,
perfectly clear, and deep,
holding the planets

and the comets,
depth after depth,
and the child

framed in her arms
like the moon
in clouds.

My mouth was hanging open
and my heart near bursting.
I never thought he'd ever …

not really ever … fall for …
And … no! I hadn't known how much
I didn't want him to

but then he takes me in his arms
even more hungrily than before.
You, my earthy queen, he says,

you are my destiny.
The stars deliver me to you
night after night.

And I burst into tears.
Actual real ones.
And we went back to bed.

CASPAR'S WIFE

The first time I saw you, Caspar,
I knew you were a good man.
I was weighed down – betrothal robes,
and jewels, and protocol,
but your hand, when you took mine,
was warm and you whispered,
There's nothing to be frightened of.

I used to lie here, in this bed,
and hear the three of you
coming down the turret stairs at dawn,
slapping each other's backs, and laughing,
and you'd come in, flushed and excited;
a man returning from the hunt,
eager to tell me how the chase had gone.
How you loved that country overhead,
the silent land you roamed in, night after night.

Do you remember that wound you had once, Caspar,
hunting in a forest? Vicious as an animal;
a parasite, leeching your life to feed its own.
I staunched its mouth
but most of all I watched it.
I must have thought my vigilance
could keep it at bay.
I willed your flesh to fight it.
I kissed your fevered face;
each kiss a prayer, a pledge
that I would always, always
be where you needed me.

And now the last,

the last thing you need from me,

I'm doing. These words you breathe

are making their way through me.

Let them not falter. Let them reach my heart,

unfurl their banners, flame

like that star burning beyond your window.

The worst wound of your life

it dealt you,

in leading you to that Jewish child.

Since then you've ached

over the loss of what you found:

something completely precious

that you jeopardised.

But, Caspar, you know, you must know,

that you came back more tender,

humbler, sweeter,

wiser,

as though you had some inner guiding star.

And now,

are these,

will these be

your final words?

Mercy

Joy

BECAUSE I HAVE BEEN COMPLACENT
ABOUT CLIMATE CHANGE

Winter is senile. He has forgotten how, in my childhood home,
my mother would sift ashes over the evening's embers,
smooring them flat with the shovel-back to keep the essential in.
He was watching her, for in the mornings I'd find a warm core
and on the inside of every windowpane the sweep of Winter's palm
where he'd breathed his dreams onto the glass and sealed them in
– his cherished paradises: hushed ice-forests, heavily, deeply rich.
Now, in December, the postman's in shorts, snow an urban myth
and Winter has bedded down with the homeless and the poor, dreamless,
bewildered, mumbling to passers-by that I abandoned him.
But how can I atone? There are no freezing drifts to trudge through
barefoot, as an emperor once did to repent his abuse of power.
I'll be a servant of the edges, to restore Winter to his right mind
and rightful sway – and my home to a time / season balance.

DECEMBER

It was the dog woke me.

I keep him chained up in the yard.

I said to the wife to do the nine, nine, nine

but you gotta sort things out yourself these days

so I creeps out – with my favourite wrench –

dodgin the security light ...

Noises from the biggest outhouse.

Get my eye to a gap in the wall

and there's this girl on her back,

a bloody baby splodgin out between her legs!

This bloke's pullin off his t-shirt to wrap it up.

They'll have scarpered from that place

the refugees are kept in. Bloody hell!

I'm in there like a shot.

Not in here you're not, I yell. But

he's gawpin at the baby. She's out of it.

Pack it in! The wife. From nowhere. *Shift yourself,*

she says to me. *We gotta keep her warm.*

She's on her mobile, to Pam-I-used-to-be-a-midwife.

What's her name? she asks the bloke

but it's something she can't catch so it's *love*, this; *love* that.

Love, it's a boy. OK? You'll be ok, love.

When I get back with a duvet an stuff, bossy Pam's already there!

She's nabbed the baby, and an actual young copper

is kneelin by the mum and the two worst tossers

from The Farmer's Arms. Who let those bastards in?

And then they're liftin the mum up, gently as they can,

onto the duvet and out into the yard.

Suddenly the bloke is on his knees.

All overcome. I say to him,

I bet you didn't mean for it all to end up here, eh?

In among the tractor parts and oil cans. Did you, eh?

He mightn't understand the words but he'll get the drift.

And then I see he's cryin, head in hands,

tears oozin between his fingers,

no shirt on – and it's free-ee-zin – head down to the floor.

I feel like kickin him but a man when he's down like that ...

I say, *Go easy, mate.*

I take my jacket off and put it round him.

Give him a shove. A shake.

Then I hold on. To him. *Hold on*, I say.

He pulls himself together. Up we stand.

I gesture he should keep my jacket

– his own cheap one and his hoodie're covered in her blood.

He looks at them, at me. I shake my head.

Tomorrow, I say. *Tomorrow.*

I see the blue lights flashin up the lane.

Come on, son. You're a father now.

Come on.

RAPT, LIKE AN ORACLE

in memory of Andrew O'Neill, Welsh musician and broadcaster

Thanes in the brilliant mead-hall, triumphing,
and all the more because they know that, outside,
Night is being slain afresh each time a blade of light
flashes from the briefly opened door.
That's what you want.
      That's what you want in the depths of winter
but when we came to the parish church,
the last Sunday evening before Christmas,
all the lights were out. Only a few candles.
Hardly Health and Safety, someone hissed.
We told each other that there'd been a power cut;
that any minute it would right itself
but still when everyone was seated – nothing.
Nothing happened. We all just sat there. Together. In the dark.

A church at night – especially at Christmas –
you expect it to be bright but here
those little, wavering flames could only nudge the darkness
and draw back. Feathery shadows fluttered in the rafters
and I was on a forest floor, a cavernous under-arch
of soughing branches shuffling scraps from a paltry moon
and Night breathing, close, about to lick my skin … and ….

A pure note, with its delicate retinue, floated out above us.
Un Seren …
We all, I swear, looked up

and he must have had more candles brought
for now light everywhere was beating back the dark,
the singing strengthening,
assuring us that *One Star* was enough,
was the only necessary one.

That's the flair he had. He could make a thing
something you'd not forget.
Died in his prime.

He also left me this: the time he was lambasting
the prejudice, hypocrisy and cant
so rampant in the Church, when he suddenly caught fire,
flared up, rapt, like an oracle, and said, in Welsh,
What I believe ... what I believe in is the ... the ...
cnewyllyn – *the kernel – love.*

Welsh:
'Un Seren' – One Star
the title of a Christmas song
composed by Delwyn Siôn

OPENING CHRISTMAS GIFTS

Christmas – celebration of the One who Saves ...
of the rescuer ... the locked door opened ...
ladder rising from the pit ... flag on the horizon ...
the whispered, *Yes*.

So we give each other presents, wrapped because
Love always must emerge,
fresh as when we first discovered it:
shy saviour of the world.

THE COST OF CHRISTMAS

A promise, given, and accepted.
Out in the darkness a horizon forms.
When, we start to say; not *If*
or worse than that, *If only.*

Time, that was a pool,
becomes a road,
acquires a destination,
and we know we're travelling.

A promise is a fragile thing,
dependent on our willingness
to put our trust in an assertion
that may never be a fact.

Fulfilment happens in obscurity
– back lane, out-house, womb –
and the arrival
is so small, so crushable

that we drop to our knees
beneath the weight
of what we realise we have assented to:
that violence is not what saves the world.

TWO PAINTINGS

BY MEMBERS OF THE GENTILESCHI FAMILY

Palazzo Blu, Pisa

AURELIO LOMI GENTILESCHI PAINTS

THE SHEPHERDS ADORE THE INFANT CHRIST, c.1588

He wants to say *heaven flung on earth*

        explosion on impact

      flesh, radiant

so, from the centre, up right across the frame

the infant blazes – a delighted star –

towards these most obscure of men

who forget – and recognise – themselves

in this implausible newborn

because we always do

– when we see the real – know it.

ARTEMISIA GENTILESCHI PAINTS
CHRIST AND THE SAMARITAN WOMAN AT THE WELL, 1636/37

Artemisia – well-named for the fleet-foot archeress
unflinching in a mist of arrows –
takes her stand square on to the well-head at noon.
Her point of view is the painting's fulcrum,
balancing the woman, on the left, and the man.
His right hand captures centre-frame – *not this water!* –
but the heel of his left is tight against his heart,
the fingers curved to a runnel, pouring.

The woman's face is Artemisia's. She is drinking him in
and I've never seen a Christ like hers, yearning
for connection, longing to be allowed to give,
sure of his value – and of hers, whatever people think.
Artemisia must have seen her uncle's *Infant Christ*;
grown him to manhood; imagined this.

And Artemisia knew men. At seventeen
– among the studio's pigments, paintbrushes, jars –
forced (just another pot, you might say, to piss in)
and tortured at the trial because a woman's word against a man's …

And she knew God: three children dead;
betrayal and abandonment. Yet here
she has him lavishing himself, hoping she'll accept him,
and as close to a mother as a man can get.

RESCUE

I didn't see the moon leaving.
My eyes were on the darkness gathering itself together
      underneath the conifers
like a foundered beggar wrapping himself in his own arms.

Nothing ventures out into the open.
The cold is set like a trap. The shocked stars look away.
Distance is kept.

Some pain, there is, like this.
To escape it we run deeper in
and call that peace.

So there had to be a night, a hillside,
throngs of angels, glory,
shepherds hurrying across the winter fields.

NADOLIG

Nos
Seren
Addewid
Cyflawniad
Tywyllwch yn llawn lleisiau
Diwedd unigrwydd

    Oíche
    Réalt
    Gealltanas
    Fíorú
    Dorchadas líonta le guthanna
    Deireadh leis an uaigneas

        Night
        A Star
        A Promise
        A Fulfilment
        Darkness filled with voices
        An end to loneliness

COMFORT AND ...

I was apprenticed to endurance
– the head held high
above the palpitating heart;

survival astonishing, and always only
till the next time. I learnt little
about joy. It seemed beside the point.

Forty years on: *You are exhausted.*
Take this and see ... A small lump of clay.
Pointless, I thought, but I obliged.

Some of my thumbprints down one side
were like the heads of people looking up.
At what?

It was December. There was silver thread to hand.
I pressed some tiny snippets into that muddy sky ...
a star.

I cried out, *It's so small. So very, very far away!*
But
that point of light ...

DECEMBER 28th

After Christmas – always – Childermas:
Slaughter of Innocents; Threat Neutralised.
The Prince of War, glistening with success,
allures us. *This*, he says, *is what you want.*
Not a stable, sheep-herding losers, a star.

THE COVENTRY CAROL

Herod the king, in his raging,
Chargid he hath this day
His men of might in his own sight
All yonge children to slay *

a paper boat
on an ocean
the weight of a baby
in your arms

out of the night
come angels
wise men
and the death squad

the dream
the nightmare
happen in the dark
hinterland of Christmas

ruthless power
strikes fast
strikes all
Childermas

inside information

flight

exile and biding time

the strategies of the escapee

who never imitates

the warlord tactics

who lets the level in the desert cistern

rise slowly, over thirty years

knowing new men of might

will smash in

achieve the kill

provoke the overflow

* from the sixteenth-century *Coventry Carol*
about The Slaughter of the Innocents, King Herod's
killing of the male infants of Bethlehem in an
attempt to obliterate his newly born rival;
commemorated on 28th December, the feast day
known as Childermas

REVOLUTION

I place this candle by the night-filled pane
to light the three kings coming from the east,
splendid in their confidence that something is beginning.

This way. This way! our glimmering windows tell them
for they come to every town as every year is dying
and swiftly word goes round that tyranny is shaken.

Our candles are whispers urging them on,
signals to each other that we haven't stopped hoping,
that our doors are ajar should the miracle choose us.

A light, an open door: our subterfuge, our revolution,
our stand against the mighty, our economy of mercy,
of kings on their knees in the presence of a child.

It is an Irish custom to place a lit
candle in a window on Christmas Eve to
guide the Three Kings to the infant Jesus,
and to leave the front door ajar in case
Mary and Joseph need a welcome.

BIRTH

After each of my deliveries
– their hallucinatory pain –
I entered into a day or two of sanctuary
in which my essential, sacred task
was to look the newly untethered
into life. The gaze
precedes, and nourishes, all other cherishing.
I marvelled on the threshold of each child,
in awe at witnessing the great world
shifted irrevocably by one small person.

After a good Christmas,
there are some days like those.
Feasted and reconciled, we are content
in a time not ruled by time.
We see that, yes, we love each other,
down to our roots.
In the marvellous glar
we will go on seeing each other
whole, and flawed, and always wonderful.

Ulster-Scots:
glar – shiny, sticky mud

NEW YEAR'S EVE, CARDIFF

Drinkers surge out of The Conway,
all embrace and ready cherishing,
kissing everyone and anyone and all
over the neighbours gathering in the road,
dodged by the teenagers aghast at the adult world,
too young to be elsewhere
and embarrassed at being with the very old,
and the weary parents clamped to a baby alarm,
and the people nobody knows who've just moved in
who are wondering how it all plays out
and we could tell them but
Now! A shout and a grabbing of hands
and everyone's Scottish, rhetorical,
Should auld acquaintance be forgot
and never brought to mind?

Each year. We mind
the faces gone into the dark,
who looked up at the Council fireworks
and pumped their arms and sang,
who flicker now on the edges of the crowd,
in the crush as the circle dance contracts
and widens; here, not here.
And we never know all the words:
We twa hae paidl'd in the burn,
frae morning sun till dine
but seas between us braid hae roar'd
sin' auld lang syne.

Looking desertion in the face,

the gaps we didn't close, love wasted,

wasted time ...

Fitting, that sad confession as we leave the year,

of how we slackened off, or worse;

of faces swimming up from depths we consigned them to;

of hurts hinged on a word we could have said.

That's why the ritual commands,

... a hand my trusty fiere!

and gie's a hand o thine!

demands we braid ourselves, pledging good will

so, on the December street

we are each other's angel choir,

promising peace, our hearts' desire.

And when the new guy shyly says,

Ah could aye gie ma pipes

a guid skirl neist year?

everyone cheers.

Scots:

aul lang syne - old long since / times long gone
fiere - friend
dine - dinnertime
skirl - a high-pitched sound;
      to play (especially of the bagpipes)
neist - next

AS THE YEAR BEGINS

for Gill and Alan

I would like my grave to be
marked not by a stone but glass:
a sturdy panel, windowing my life
in a mosaic of seeing / seeing-through.

Here, in a piece of most particular – almost royal – blue,
won't you remember
how, from a height,
we watched the unhurried, strategizing sea
re-take the estuary plain,
spreading, in ever-widening fans,
a rippled, supple mirror for the cloudless sky,
and how we plunged
to stride out to its quick
where water, headlands, seal-black cliffs
and sunlight sang on one note?
We knew our luck, that day.

In another pane would be
a bud of densest white
burning against brown,
flaring in orange up to an indigo sky,
to a blackness tinkled with pin-prick stars,
for that November night on a cwm's flank,
so mild it was *maes yr haf*

and our fire leapt

mostly for joy

at being in the dark, alive.

And then a roundel,

bisected by a silver line,

pearl-pink above a smudge of grey,

for all my precious after-sorrow dawns.

So, passing, anyone might say,

This grave is bright.

What must the life have been?

Welsh:
cwm - narrow valley
maes yr haf - summer meadow

WORSHIP IN WINTER, WALES

In darkness, any light is LIGHT;

a spark is FIRE; the smallest gleam is SUN

so oil and wick and wax and twinkling bulbs

declare defiance of the grave

and welcome for that *golau arall* /other light

by which we see the stars,

and for the womb's lightlessness

and imagination's cave.

We honour light. We honour necessary darkness.

We honour reconciliation of all things.

Welsh:

golau arall – another (kind of) light
from the Welsh song, *Ar Hyd Y Nos* / All Through The Night:

Golau arall yw tywyllwch
I arddangos gwir brydferthwch
Teulu'r nefoedd mewn tawelwch
Ar hyd y nos.

Darkness is another kind of light
To display to us the true beauty
Of the family of the heavens in silence
All through the night.

NEW YEAR'S DAY

Mothering the year you usher me
to the nest's rim where I
– all fledgling – flutter, flail and fall
into the future. No going back.

And we say time is a river.
We curate its eddies into days,
dam it up as months and reach,
on Old Year's Night, a precipice;
another metaphor of brink and flow.

And we make time cyclical,
seizing on the seasons' wheel and return
as licence to expect repeated
new beginnings for ourselves.

But *fall* or *flow* or *cycle* –
nothing hits home like *arrow*,
fletched in every moment
for its flight straight to eternity,
time's target, time's frame.

The god of new beginnings is the one for me
since I hardly know what it is I'm doing
– how much damage, how much good –
so I choose forgiveness and forgiven-ness and hope.